STUDIO SERIES™ BY PETER PAUPER PRESS

D1609086

Blessed

ARTIST'S COLORING BOOK

PETER PAUPER PRESS, INC.
Rye Brook, NY

PETER PAUPER PRESS
Fine Books and Gifts Since 1928

OUR STORY

In 1928, at the age of twenty-two, Peter Beilenson began printing books on a small press in the basement of his parents' home in Larchmont, New York. Peter—and later, his wife, Edna—sought to create fine books that sold at "prices even a pauper could afford."

Today, still family owned and operated, Peter Pauper Press continues to honor our founders' legacy—and our customers' expectations—of beauty, quality, and value.

Images used under license from Shutterstock.com

Designed by Margaret Rubiano

Copyright © 2023
Peter Pauper Press, Inc.
3 International Drive
Rye Brook, NY 10573 USA

Published in the United Kingdom and Europe by
Peter Pauper Press, Inc., c/o White Pebble International
Units 2-3, Spring Business Park
Stanbridge Road
Havant, Hampshire PO9 2GJ, UK

All rights reserved
ISBN 978-1-4413-4084-9
Printed in China

7 6 5 4 3

www.peterpauper.com

If you color with markers, place a piece of scrap paper behind your coloring page to protect the next page.

YOUR WORD IS A LAMP TO MY FEET
AND A LIGHT TO MY PATH

PSALM 119:105 (NASB)

My hope is
in you
all day long

PSALM 25:5 (NIV)

My soul magnifies the LORD

Luke 1:46 (RSV)

I am
with you
ALWAYS

Matthew 28:20 (RSV)

BE KIND TO ONE ANOTHER

EPHESIANS 4:32 (NKJV)

AS I HAVE LOVED YOU, SO YOU MUST LOVE ONE ANOTHER

John 13:34 (NIV)

Fix Your Thoughts on what is True, and honorable, and right

Philippians 4:8 (NLT)

I AM FEARFULLY AND WONDERFULLY MADE

Psalm 139:14 (NKJV)

Lift up your voice

ISAIAH 40:9 (RSV)

A wonderful future awaits those who LOVE PEACE

Psalm 37:37 (NLT)

WHOEVER LIVES
IN LOVE
LIVES IN GOD,
AND GOD IN THEM

1 John 4:16 (NIV)

Let's not get tired of doing what is good

GALATIANS 6:9 (NLT)

She laughs
without fear
OF THE
FUTURE

Proverbs 31:25 (NLT)

Be joyful in hope, patient in affliction, faithful in prayer

Romans 12:12 (NIV)

Store your
treasures
in heaven

MATTHEW 6:20 (NLT)

LOVE your neighbor as yourself

Mark 12:31 (RSV)

Those who seek the LORD lack no good thing

PSALM 34:10 (RSV)

DO NOT FEAR,
for I am
with you

Isaiah 41:10 (NASB)

I AM THE WAY, THE TRUTH, AND THE LIFE

JOHN 14:6 (NKJV)

Be strong and courageous

Joshua 1:9 (NASB)

Do not let your heart be troubled

John 14:1 (NASB)

Don't let anyone look down on you because YOU ARE YOUNG

1 Timothy 4:12 (NIV)

LET US NOT LOVE WITH WORDS OR SPEECH BUT WITH ACTIONS AND IN TRUTH

1 John 3:18 (NIV)

WHEN I AM AFRAID,

I will put my

trust in You

Psalm 56:3 (nasb)

The LORD bless you, and keep you

Numbers 6:24 (NASB)